Against the Tommies

Tommies

History of 26 Reserve Division 1914 - 1918

David Bilton

Pen & Sword
MILITARY

First published in Great Britain in 2016 by
PEN & SWORD MILITARY
An imprint of
Pen & Sword Books Ltd
47 Church Street
Barnsley, South Yorkshire
S70 2AS

ISBN 978 1 47383 3 678

Printed and bound in England
By CPI Group (UK) Ltd, Croydon, CR0 4YY

Pen & Sword Books Ltd incorporates the Imprints of Aviation, Atlas,
Family History, Fiction, Maritime, Military, Discovery, Politics, History,
Archaeology, Select, Wharncliffe Local History, Wharncliffe True Crime,
Military Classics, Wharncliffe Transport, Leo Cooper, The Praetorian Press,
Remember When, Seaforth Publishing and Frontline Publishing.

For a complete list of Pen & Sword titles please contact
PEN & SWORD BOOKS LIMITED
47 Church Street, Barnsley, South Yorkshire, S70 2AS, England
E-mail: enquiries@pen-and-sword.co.uk
Website: www.pen-and-sword.co.uk

Contents

Preface

This book is based on the divisional history of the 26th (Württemberg) Reserve Division, the staff of which compiled and published a record of its service in 1920. The text and photos chronologically illustrate life behind and in the trenches for the men and officers of the division.

What makes German wartime histories different from the many published by Allied forces is the large number of photographs included, all of them taken by soldiers in the field. As cameras were relatively expensive, many of the photos were taken by officers but this does not detract from the story the images tell.

Keeping diaries and taking photographs were forbidden to Allied troops, but until very late in the war there were no such restrictions in the German Army. Most things were uncensored: this permitted the production of accounts, during and after the war, that reflect what the German soldier saw and experienced, warts and all, in every theatre. As well as giving a clear picture of what the front line and the area behind looked like, it also documented the changes brought about by Allied shelling and provides new images for well-known villages and towns. What is especially interesting for British readers is that this division spent a considerable part of its war fighting against British troops, particularly during the Somme and Third Ypres. As a result much of what is portrayed is familiar but, at the same time, different.

I have kept most of the photographs from the original book. Some of these are mundane, but this is the quality which enables them to tell the real story of life then and there. The text retains the same sections, headings and order as the original book though it has been edited. In attempting to maintain a German point of view, I have truncated much of the original to highlight the detail but left German place names, while adding material to explain and enhance. As a result the narrative is a mixture of translation (deliberately in the style of the original), reduction and addition.

The original text starts with a quote, from Hindenburg, about how good the division was. Does this correspond with Allied army intelligence reports and how did it compare with its senior sister division, the 26th (Regular) Division? Intelligence reports for 1917 state that it was a very good division, of a combative value equal to that of the majority of the active (regular) divisions. The report for 1918 is not as glowing but still good. It was rated a first-class division, that could be depended upon and on the whole fought well, but it did not distinguish itself in any way. When this intelligence is compared with 26th Division, the senior regular unit, the 26th Reserve fared well. In 1917 Allied intelligence reported that the regular division had conducted itself well though morale was weak later in the year. However, during 1918 it was a first-class division.

Hindenburg was correct in his summation. Even in a deteriorating situation, the Württemberg divisions were both top quality fighting units with good reason to be proud of their service.

David Bilton
September 2015

Acknowledgements

As always a great big thank you to Anne Coulson for checking the manuscript.

Part One
From the beginning of the war
until the end of 1916

'All contingents did their duty. Each had good and less good divisions;
Württemberg alone had only good.'

Erich Ludendorff
(My War Memories, 1914-1918)

Unlike her sister division, the 26th (Württemberg) Regular Division, the 26th (Württemberg) Reserve division fought only on the Western Front, first against the French and then against the British. In four and a half years of bitter fighting, in some of the most violent battles of the war, it distinguished itself both at home, where it was highly regarded, and with its enemy.

1. Leaving for the Front

The division was formed in the first days of August 1914 at different locations across Württemberg. Consisting of three reserve infantry regiments (IR), 119, 120 and 121, the Württemberg Reserve Dragoon Regiment and Reserve Field Artillery Regiment 26, the division was composed of reserve and militia men.

To this were added two active service units, Infantry Regiment 180 from Tübingen and 4.Feld Pioneer Komp.13. An extra regiment, Reserve Infantry Regiment 99, was formed in Alsace and went to the Bruche Valley, while the regular regiment went to Sainte-Marie-aux-Mines. The first Divisional Commander was General der Infanterie, Freiherr von Soden, and the Commanders of 51 Reserve Infantry Brigade and 52 Reserve Infantry Brigade were Generalleutnant von Wundt and Generalleutnant von Auwärter respectively.

After detraining around 10 August, between Freiburg and Neubreisgau, the division joined 28 Reserve Division, from Baden. The two divisions formed the new XIV Reserve Korps, part of 7.Armee, commanded by Generaloberst Josias von Heeringen which had been formed at the outbreak of the war. It formed the extreme left (southern) wing of the German armies on the Western Front and during the execution of the French Plan XVII, the mobilisation plan of the French

Army, 7.Armee covered Alsace, successfully repulsing the French attack in the Battle of Lorraine.

II. The Vosges campaign
August and September 1914

By 9 August, ahead of the rest of the division, IR 180 had received its baptism of fire at Markirch. On 18 August the division penetrated the Vosges and drove the French in a series of bitter battles – at Grendelbruch, at Donon in Rothau and Dijon – over the River Meurthe. Saint-Dié-des-Vosges was occupied on 27 August, and pursuit of the French continued with tough forest fighting towards Épinal.

For strategic reasons the division was withdrawn on 11 September and marched to Saarburg, where they were greeted, on 17 September, by the King of Württemberg, Wilhelm II. Leaving Saarburg, the division marched to Saint-Avold and then to Hargarten where they entrained from 22 September for an unknown destination in northern France – the Somme.

III. The fighting in the engagement in the north of France
End of September and October 1914

The division, now part of 2.Armee, moved through Trier to Liège and was filmed moving westward through Namur and Valenciennes. From 25 September it was stationed in the Cambrai region.

On 27 September, Bapaume was captured and the front advanced towards Albert. Pozières, Thiepval, Ovillers, La Boisselle were taken by assault but constant French reinforcements around Albert held the advance and the town did not fall.

As a result of the French action, the division held positions on both sides of the Ancre forming a line: Beaumont – Saint-Pierre Divion – Thiepval – Ovillers – La Boisselle. Both sides then dug in and the division took part in no major actions until the Somme offensive.

IV. Enemy assaults against
October 1914 to January 1915

The French tried repeatedly to regain the lost territory but were repulsed. A particularly strong attack on 29 October against Beaumont made some progress but was eventually checked by Reserve Infantry Regiment 99.

On 17 December the French attacked Ovillers from the forest of Authuille but were again repulsed, this time by Reserve Infantry Regiment 119 and Reserve Field

Artillery Regiment 26, and in the period before Christmas a further French attack against La Boisselle was also held. The fight for Granathof by Reserve Infantry Regiment 120 became famous in the German Army. During this battle mine warfare began in the sector.

V. The war of position on both sides of the Ancre
January to June 1915

January 1915 was a period of adjustment for both sides. This stationary war meant digging in. For the men of the division it was a time of hard work and 'tenacious perseverance' in mud and water during an ammunition shortage. Newly-won positions were reinforced, firstly in a long thin line, but gradually the primitive holes in the ground became a structured system of deep trenches with well designed deep dugouts and wire obstacles. These became famous during the British attacks during the Somme battles.

On 10 March, Reserve Infantry Regiment 120 was transferred to the newly formed 58th Division. During April, after renewed fighting in Thiepval Forest, the King visited the front for the second time to express his appreciation for his division's successful efforts. Assisted by 29.Landwehr Infantry Brigade and Landwehr Battalion IV/75 from Bremen, the line was successfully expanded. In May, part of the division was detached for service on the Arras front and fought at Neuville-Saint-Vaast, while in June some units of Reserve Infantry Regiment 99 and Infantry Regiment 180 took part in the battles in Le Labyrinthe at Arras. All units returned in July to the division, which was holding the Bapaume sector.

VI. The Serre battles
7-19 June 1915

The exposed positions at Toutvent-Ferme, south of Hébuterne, resulted in French attacks in the direction of Serre, particularly at the junction where the 26th Reserve Division met the neighbouring division. During one heavy attack, the adjacent division lost its footing in Toutvent-Ferme, but Reserve Infantry Regiment 119 managed to hold its positions. The situation was saved only by the rapid intervention of reserves from the 26th Reserve Division (III Battalion Infantry Regiment 180 and parts of Reserve Infantry Regiment 121), the excellent co-operation between infantry and artillery preventing a deep penetration. Infantry Regiment 180, in conjunction with 185.Infantry Brigade and a Bavarian Regiment, managed to prevent a further French advance by sealing off the area to the west of Serre by creating new positions on both sides of the road from Serre to Mailly.

VII. The continuation of positional warfare
From June 1915 to the Somme battle

The second half of the year was quieter but this changed in July when the English replaced the French. These new troops were looked upon as beginners and not highly rated at first. To improve offensive spirit, numerous regimentally competitive raids, large and small, were carried out against the new arrivals and these provided information about the British troops. On 31 January, King Wilhelm II made a third visit to the division.

In the spring of 1916 British attack preparations were detected and appropriate countermeasures initiated. Flying activity increased considerably and almost daily fierce air battles played out over Bapaume. Everyone expected an attack.

VIII. The Battle of the Somme
June to October 1916

From 24 June the enemy bombarded our positions from Serre to Ovillers with an unprecedented amount of ammunition. The bombardment was so heavy it rattled windows and doors in the back areas.

After seven days of bombardment, early on the morning of 1 July, the long awaited attack began. At least six English (sic) divisions moved against a thinly-occupied twelve kilometre front held by 26th Reserve Division on both sides of the Ancre. But nowhere were they able to break through. Many thousands of dead Englishmen lay before the front of the division. Any isolated small successes were quickly ironed out. A further large-scale attack against Ovillers was bloodily repulsed by Infantry Regiment 180. Schwaben Redoubt was lost but recaptured later in the day. On 6 July, the Divisional Commander was able to report to the King: 'All positions held completely'.

On 26 September, Thiepval was lost in a heroic battle, in which the enemy used the first tanks; the brave garrison was buried under the rubble of the lost village. The defence of Thiepval gained the admiration of the British attackers. In mid-October the bulk of the division was pulled out of the 'hell of the Somme' but some were still there fighting in November. On October 19, in Saint-Léger, they were thanked by the Kaiser. During this period casualties were heavy: total losses on the Somme amounted to 10,042 men with 99 Reserve Infantry Regiment losing 48 officers and 2,070 men.

IX The new position south of Arras
Croisilles Sector – October to end of 1916

From 10 October 1916, the bulk of the division was moved, without being rested, to the quieter Blairville – Ransart – Monchy-le-Preux position, south of Arras, where the regiments were moved between brigades. During this period many patrols were carried out to instil an offensive spirit and units on the Monchy front were particularly busy. 'Welded together with blood and iron, and raised awareness of victories, the Division prepared for new tasks.'

On December 18, the Divisional Commander was promoted to Corps Commander and replaced by Generalleutnant z. D. Albert Hermann von Fritsch.

ATT_14_002. Field service in the courtyard of the large infantry barracks in Stuttgart before the troops left for the border, 7 August 1914.

ATT_14_003. On the way to the front. Having a wash in Gengen Brook.

ATT_14_001. General of Infantry Freiherr von Soden, Commander of 26th Reserve Division 1914 - 1916.

ATT_14_006/006a (Left) A battalion of Reserve Field Artillery Regiment 26 in pursuit of the French on 'La Hongrie' near Grendelbruch Schirmeck in Alsace. (Right) Dead French soldiers after the fighting on La Hongrie on 19 August 1914.

ATT_14_004. Benfeld in Alsace on 13 August 1914 when the division passed through.

ATT_14_005. Oberehnheim in Alsace on 16/17 August 1914.

ATT_14_007. Casualties at a field gun of 1 Detachment (Bornemann) of Reserve Field Artillery Regiment 26 at Fréconrupt. They were killed by French artillery firing from Mont Donon, the highest peak in the Vosges.

ATT_14_008. French PoWs being transported east across the bridge over the Bruche River at Schirmeck on 21 August 1914.

ATT_14_009/009a. (Left) French PoWs being escorted through Saint-Dié-des-Vosges during August. (Right) Saint-Dié from the surrounding heights during August/September 1914.

ATT_14_010. On 26 August, Brigade Wundt marched through Saint-Dié. The photo clearly shows the hilly conditions of the Vosges campaign. In the distance are the Bois d'Ormont and Spitzemberg, a peak of 641 metres.

ATT_14_011. On the march against Saint-Dié. The shelling of Saint-Jean d'Ormond-Ban de Sapt during the attack by Brigade Auwärter on 26/27 August 1914.

ATT_14_012. Station Square in Saint-Dié showing the Hotel Terminus.

ATT_14_014. A house in La Bolle, set on fire by French artillery.

ATT_14_013. German artillery passing through the Les Tiges area of Saint-Dié sometime in late August or early September.

ATT_14_015. Members of 4.Kompanie Reserve Infantry Regiment 120 inspecting a French gun captured near La Bolle on 4 September 1914.

ATT_14_016. The lonely grave of a German officer killed in the fighting near Parux in the Cirey region in September.

ATT_14_017. French civilians selling food to German troops on their way to Belgium during September.

ATT_14_018. On 25 September 1914, 26th Reserve Division arrived at Cambrai.

ATT_14_019. The Kaiser in Bapaume on 29 September 1914.

ATT_14_020. Martinpuich church in September 1914, barely touched by the war.

ATT_14_022. A partially ruined sugar factory near Courcelette.

ATT_14_021. The divisional HQ, during September/October was the Café National near Courcelette.

ATT_14_023. French soldiers captured during the fighting around Thiepval – Ovillers – La Boisselle on 29 September 1914.

ATT_14_025. Thiepval Château after Infantry Regiment 180 had passed through the area on 28 September 1914.

ATT_14_024. Thiepval church.

ATT_14_026. A view of Pozières church taken during October.

ATT_14_027. During October Thiepval Château suffered considerable damage from French artillery shelling. Compare this with the photo on the previous page.

ATT_14_028. Irles church in September.

ATT_14_029. Miraumont viewed from the road to Courcelette.

ATT_14_030. French PoWs taken during the fighting for Miraumont in September 1914.

ATT_14_031. Beauregard Farm and a lonely grave being viewed by two officers of the division.

ATT_14_032. Divisional staff at Ferme Baillescourt in Miraumont during October 1914.

ATT_14_034. Oberst Grall, commander of Reserve Infantry Regiment 99, in front of Beaucourt Château.

ATT_14_033. A mill destroyed by French shellfire somewhere near Miraumont. The photo was taken in October.

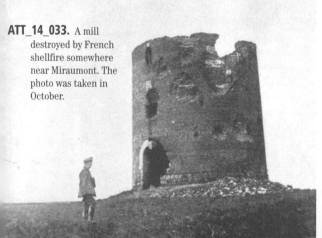

ATT_14_035. The hastily dug positions of 3 Battalion Reserve Artillery Regiment 26 near Beaucourt in October 1914.

ATT_14_036. Beaumont after the battle had moved on.

ATT_14_037. The church in Saint-Pierre Divion showing some shell damage.

ATT_14_038. A field gun of 6 Battalion Reserve Artillery Regiment 26 in position in Thiepval Château park.

ATT_14_040/040a. (Above) The front position on the outskirts of Ovillers in October 1914. (Right) The machine gun position and dugout.

ATT_14_041/041a. (Below right) The church in Ovillers after the French bombardments during October. (Below left) The Ovillers church bell was removed and placed in a divisional memorial in the village cemetery.

ATT_14_039. German officer standing in a shallow trench in front of Thiepval church in late 1914.

ATT_14_042/042a. (Below) The beginnings of trench and underground shelter construction shown in October near Ovillers. (Right) The divisional commander in a forward position talking to a soldier of Reserve Infantry Regiment 119.

ATT_14_043. Pictured in November 1914, the ruins of La Boisselle church destroyed by French artillery.

ATT_14_044. The Granathof, a French farm fought over for some considerable time, in October 1914. The view is taken in the direction of the road from La Boisselle to Albert.

ATT_14_046/046a. Field stables in the ruins of Pozières in October 1914.

ATT_14_045. The combat shelter of Reserve Infantry Regiment 120 in La Boisselle taken in November 1914.

ATT_14_049. Ovillers church bell hung as part of a German memorial in the grounds of Miraumont Château.

ATT_14_048. Joan of Arc statue in Miraumont church.

ATT_14_047. Mouquet Farm was used as a combat shelter by Reserve Infantry Regiment 121.

ATT_14_051. German artillery positions on the road Pozières – Ovillers.

ATT_14_050. French soldiers captured during their attack on the positions held by Reserve Infantry Regiment 119 in Ovillers on 17 December 1914.

ATT_14_052. 'A dashing patrol leader': Vizefeldwebel Böcker of 6 Kompanie Reserve Infantry Regiment 119 pictured in late 1914. He was killed in action near Beaumont on 9 April 1916. Before the war he was an opera singer.

ATT_14_053. French rifles captured by Reserve Infantry Regiment 119 during the French attack on their positions on 17 December 1914.

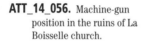

ATT_14_054. During the rains of winter 1914/1915, the trenches turned into ditches.

ATT_14_056. Machine-gun position in the ruins of La Boisselle church.

ATT_14_055/055a. (Above) By January 1915 the church at La Boisselle was a complete ruin. (Left) Vizefeldwebel Parnemann, of 4.Kompanie, Pioneer Battalion 13, in a forward position at La Boisselle.

ATT_14_057. An observation post outside La Boisselle. Note the soldier is not wearing a pickelhaube but a cloth cover that blends with the trench top.

ATT_14_058. A look-out in a forward sap near La Boisselle.

ATT_14_059. The regimental pioneer park near La Boisselle with a steadily increasing stock pile of wooden planks.

ATT_14_060. A view of the military cemetery in Miraumont after its inauguration in December 1914.

ATT_14_061/061a. Divisional artillery in a hollow outside Beaucourt.

ATT_14_063. A 21cm mortar positioned in the cemetery at Grandcourt. This gun was the standard field piece of the army and by the end of war had fired around seven million shells.

ATT_14_062. The steeple of the church in Albert. It was shelled because the Germans believed it was being used as an observation post for artillery spotters.

ATT_14_066. Construction of the 'Leiling-tunnel' in the top of Leiling gulley south of Beaumont. Leiling was the name of the officer in command of a company in Infantry Regiment 99.

ATT_14_064. Initially there were few anti-aircraft guns and divisions had to make their own. This illustrates one makeshift attempt to provide artillery fire against aircraft. This is a Light Field gun 7.7cm FK 96 held precariously in position on thick wooden planking.

ATT_14_065. A photo of the Ancre Valley in early 1915.

ATT_14_067. A well-constructed position in the swampy region of the Ancre near Saint-Pierre Divion in March 1915.

ATT_14_068. Hauptmann Leiling, after whom the tunnel was named, commanded 14 Kompanie, Reserve Infantry Regiment 99 until his death near Cambrai.

ATT_14_069. The road from Saint-Pierre Divion to Authuille.

ATT_14_070. A member of Hauptmann Leiling's Company with his commander. The trench construction method is clearly shown.

ATT_14_071. The road from Thiepval to Saint-Pierre Divion seen from the barricade blocking the road.

ATT_14_072. The front position in Thiepval Park's grounds. Probably not that dangerous in early 1915, as the men have washing hanging across it.

ATT_14_073. Thiepval Château in Spring 1915.

ATT_14_074. Thiepval Château six months later in the autumn of 1915.

ATT_14_075. The destroyed château provided the troops with considerable protection. These men are standing outside a shelter created in the damage.

ATT_14_076. Running alongside a road through Thiepval was Schwaben trench.

ATT_14_077. French XI Corps men taken prisoner in the fighting on 10/11/1915 when Brigade Wundt had attacked French positions around Beaumont-Hamel and Thiepval Wood. General Leutnant von Wundt, commander of 51.Reserve Infantry Brigade, is fifth from left, marked with x at the bottom of his coat.

ATT_14_078. The quarry near Mouquet Farm in use as a shelter.

ATT_14_079. The King of Württemberg was a regular visitor to his troops. This is the march past of Infantry Regiment 180 on 13 April 1915, when he visited the division.

ATT_14_081. Monument to General Faidherbe, who won several small victories against the Prussian First Army at the towns of Ham, Hallue, Pont-Noyelles, and Bapaume during the Franco-Prussian War, in front of Bapaume Town Hall.

ATT_14_080/080a. (Below) After the march past, the King visited the soldiers' cemetery in Miraumont. (Right) A humorous mock memorial in Miraumont over a mass grave for the louse.

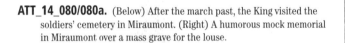

ATT_14_082. Bapaume church.

ATT_14_083/083a. (Above) The courtyard of a field hospital in Bapaume. (Below) Men of the divisional train enjoying a beer during the loading of provisions in Bapaume.

Wurttemberger Hof

ATT_14_084. Recovery ward in a Bapaume field hospital.

ATT_14_085. Keeping a division in the field required considerable logistical support. A large town like Bapaume provided the space and facilities for corps troops to provide essential services for the fighting man. This is a field bakery somewhere in Bapaume.

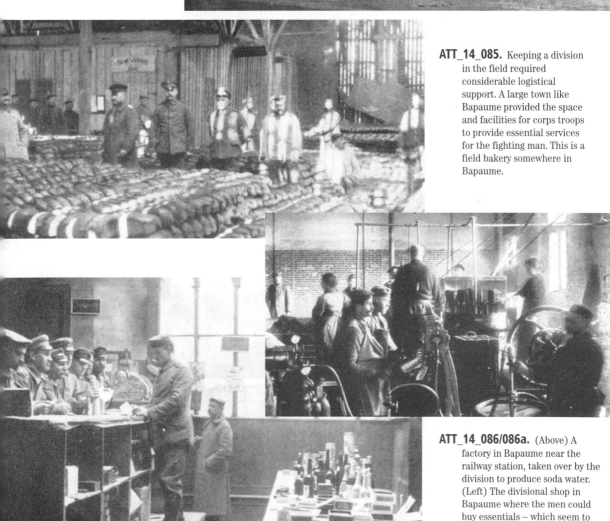

ATT_14_086/086a. (Above) A factory in Bapaume near the railway station, taken over by the division to produce soda water. (Left) The divisional shop in Bapaume where the men could buy essentials – which seem to be alcohol and tobacco.

ATT_14_087. An army marches on its stomach: the divisional butchers was near Warlencourt on the road to Bapaume.

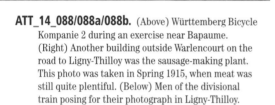

ATT_14_088/088a/088b. (Above) Württemberg Bicycle Kompanie 2 during an exercise near Bapaume. (Right) Another building outside Warlencourt on the road to Ligny-Thilloy was the sausage-making plant. This photo was taken in Spring 1915, when meat was still quite plentiful. (Below) Men of the divisional train posing for their photograph in Ligny-Thilloy.

ATT_14_089. Taken in July 1915, this photo clearly shows the damage sustained by Puisieux Château during the earlier fighting.

ATT_14_090. La Louvière, after the fighting around Serre in June 1915.

ATT_14_091. Major Freiherr von Meerscheidt-Hüllessem, commander of 1.Battalion Reserve Infantry Regiment 99, in the Heidenkopf position after the fighting at Serre in June 1915.

ATT_14_092. Soldiers of Infantry Regiment 180 in the 'Duck's bill' in the Heidenkopf position, just three metres from the enemy positions.

ATT_14_094. The hand grenade troop of Reserve Infantry Regiment 119.

ATT_14_093. Two men of Reserve Infantry Regiment 119 repairing the first trench to the north of Beaumont. The damage was caused during the fighting around Serre.

ATT_14_095. New positions used after the Serre fighting in June. This road runs from Serre to Mailly.

ATT_14_096. In the trenches of 1.Battalion Reserve Infantry Regiment 119 near Beaumont. Pictured are Hauptmann von Breuning (right) and Vizefeldwebel Wenz, a successful patrol leader.

ATT_14_098. Four soldiers in the summer of 1915, showing the newly issued gas protection equipment – a primitive gas mask.

ATT_14_097. Food carriers taking rations to the men in the front line.

ATT_14_099. Sergeant Böcker's patrol on the slope just in front of the enemy's position north of Beaumont-Hamel.

ATT_14_100/100a. (Right) A temporary accommodation and work area – Kolonie Beaumont-Sud. (Below) A view from the front trenches of Beaumont in the distance.

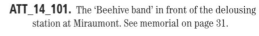

ATT_14_101. The 'Beehive band' in front of the delousing station at Miraumont. See memorial on page 31.

ATT_14_102. The Ancre in the summer of 1915.

ATT_14_104. The first 'English' soldier, captured on 13 August 1915, belonged to 1 Royal Irish Fusiliers.

ATT_14_103. The Reading Hall in Miraumont. Marked with an X is Private Nowowiejski, who in civilian life was a professional pianist.

ATT_14_106. Sports day in Miraumont. The crowd are waiting for the first competitor to grab the sausage while standing on a rotating beam.

ATT_14_105. The mill at Miraumont was used by the divisional quartermaster and was in full operation during August 1916.

ATT_14_107. Making charcoal in Grévillers forest for use in dug-out cookers.

ATT_14_108. An infantry Earth Mortar dug in behind the front line, a large trench mortar which threw a heavy bomb a short distance. They were called Earth or Albrecht Mortars to differentiate them from the other type of heavy mortar manned by the artillery.

ATT_14_109. The mill at Pozières in Spring 1915.

ATT_14_110. A peaceful view of Achiet-le-Petit.

ATT_14_112. By May 1916, the mill at Pozières was a ruin.

ATT_14_111. The mill at Pozières in September 1915.

ATT_14_113. Memorial service in the soldiers' cemetery in Miraumont on All Souls' Day 1915.

ATT_14_114. When the church graveyard was full, a new soldiers' cemetery was started nearby. By November 1915 there had been many interments.

ATT_14_115. With most French farmers away with the army, the only able-bodied men around to help were the German soldiers. Here they are seen using a threshing machine.

ATT_14_116. A German mine exploding under enemy positions in Authuille Wood in December 1915.

ATT_14_117/117a. (Right) Charcoal makers in the forest at Grévillers in 1915. (Below) A view of Grévillers.

ATT_14_118. The commander of 52.Reserve Infantry Brigade, General von Auwärter, discussing company exercises on 1 March 1916.

ATT_14_120. Gefreiters Sommer and Guberan (4.Kompanie Reserve Infantry Regiment 121) after the award of the Iron Cross 1st Class for bold, successful patrols. Behind is the Company Commander Captain Baron von Ziegesar, who was killed near Beaumont during the Somme battles of 1916.

ATT_14_119. Leutnant Gustav Leffers of Feld-Flieger Detachment 132 in front of one of his victims in January 1916. He was shot down and died, aged 21, on 27 December 1916.

ATT_14_121. Conscripted French workers repairing roads behind the front. They are repairing the road between Bihucourt to Biefvillers.

ATT_14_122/122a. (Left) The arrival of the King of Württemberg in Bapaume on 31 January 1916, for one of his regular visits to the front. (Below) Captured by a patrol of Infantry Regiment 180 west of Serre, Lancashire Fusiliers are marched through Grévillers on their way to divisional headquarters for interrogation.

ATT_14_123/123a. (Above) Grévillers in 1916. (Right) The third visit of the King of Württemberg on 31 January 1916, to the men of the division. On this visit he gave out medals for bravery and good service.

ATT_14_124/124a. (Left) On 31 January 1916, during his third visit to the division, he visited the military cemetery in Miraumont. (Below) A trench-fighting demonstration for the King of Württemberg during his January visit.

ATT_14_125/125a. In 1916 Divisional Staff quarters were situated in a château in Biefvillers. (Right) Grévillers in the winter of 1915/16.

ATT_14_126. Patrol Scheidel from 3.Kompanie Reserve Infantry Regiment 119 were praised by the divisional commander on 28 March 1916, for successful work.

ATT_14_127. Biefvillers in March 1916.

ATT_14_128/128a. On 21 March 1916, the division was visited by members of the Stuttgart Court Theatre.

ATT_14_130. The narrow gauge railway connected Irles to Miraumont and Beaumont. It was used to transport materials to the pioneer park.

ATT_14_129. The collection point and dump at the pioneer park in Irles.

ATT_14_131. Field railway construction in the artillery hollow at Beaucourt in Spring 1916.

ATT_14_132. A 25cm trench mortar crew pose in a mortar pit with their weapon, near the front line.

ATT_14_133. A 10cm Ring cannon, a wheeled artillery piece used by field artillery units.

ATT_14_134/134a. 'English' PoWs being fed after capture on 6 April 1916, by 'Barbarians'. Behind them is a field cooker. (Below) Soldiers of the South Wales Borderers taken prisoner on 7 April 1916, are being marched through Grévillers shortly after their capture.

ATT_14_138. On the right, in front of a plane shot down near Courcelette by a German Fokker, is the Commanding Officer of XIV. Reserve Corps, Generalleutnant von Stein, who later In the year became Minister of War. On the left, with walking stick, is Generalleutnant von Wundt, commander of 51.Reserve Infantry Brigade.

ATT_14_137. The regimental commanders of the division together at a meeting in May 1916.

ATT_14_136. In April 1916 the divisional commander presented bravery awards to some of the men of Battalion von Ellrichshausen, II.Battalion Reserve Infantry Regiment 119.

ATT_14_135. The spoils: helmets, guns and rifles, after the repulse of an 'English' patrol near Beaumont on 30 April 1916.

ATT_14_139. The new soldiers' cemetery at Miraumont in May 1916. The memorial is still under construction.

ATT_14_140. A barricade, pictured in May 1916, was constructed in Serre along the road to Puisieux. This allowed free movement without British observation.

ATT_14_141. Peeling potatoes for the unit's cooker somewhere in Serre.

ATT_14_142. A trench scene, south of Serre, showing normal trench living for men of Infantry Regiment 180.

ATT_14_144. Looking out from the front line trench west of Beaumont at Auchonvillers.

ATT_14_143. A pioneer dump in an area known as the 'Fünf Weiden' (five willows), north east of Beaucourt.

ATT_14_145/145a. Hauptmann Künlen of Reserve Infantry Regiment 119 with his aides. He was killed in August 1918, whilst fighting on the Somme for the third time. (Below) Entitled 'Trench life', the photo clearly shows the sturdy and well-planned construction of the German trenches on the Somme.

ATT_14_146. Enjoying a midday meal in the forward trenches.

ATT_14_148. On the left is the commander of Reserve Feld Artillery Brigade 26, General von Maur, who took over the brigade in June after serving on the Eastern Front. The unknown officer on the right is his adjutant.

ATT_14_147. The destruction to a trench west of Beaumont caused by 'English' shelling on 1 May 1916.

ATT_14_149. Shelters in a wood in Beaumont.

ATT_14_151. Major Schäfer, commanding officer of III. Battalion Reserve Infantry Regiment 119, with two brave patrol leaders.

ATT_14_150. 'Die Kolonie' (The Colony), was a semi-permanent troop accommodation constructed into a hillside south of Beaumont. The photo was taken in May 1916.

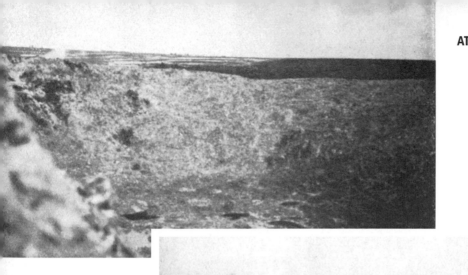

ATT_14_152. Mine crater 30m in diameter and 12m depth, which initiated the British attacks on 1 July, against the division in the trenches near Beaumont.

ATT_14_153. A view from the German trenches of the battlefield to the west of Beaumont.

ATT_14_154. Battalion shelters and soldiers' cemetery in Beaumont.

ATT_14_155. A visit from the Brigade Commander. He is inspecting the area occupied by Reserve Infantry Regiment 119.

ATT_14_156. The front line trenches west of Beaumont after repair and removal of debris caused by the battle.

ATT_14_157. A British plane shot down on 1 July, over German lines.

ATT_14_158. Another view of trench life, including the use of a trench periscope to view British lines.

ATT_14_159. The commander and adjutant of Reserve Infantry Regiment 119 outside their headquarters during the Somme battles.

ATT_14_161. How Beaumont looked on 2 July 1916: apart from shell-blasted trees, there is nothing else in view.

ATT_14_160. Beaumont after six days of British preparatory artillery fire before the Somme battle.

ATT_14_162. The remains of Beaucourt mill after the initial bombardment.

ATT_14_165. The headquarters of Reserve Infantry Regiment 121 after British artillery fire before the battle.

ATT_14_163. The results of British artillery fire on the Ancre light railway.

ATT 14 164. Major Prager of Bavarian Reserve Infantry Regiment 8 in Saint-Pierre Divion on 5 July 1916.

ATT_14_166. Thiepval Château on 16 July 1916.

ATT_14_167. The damage sustained by Beaucourt Manor House during the British bombardment is clearly shown by this photo taken on 16 August.

ATT_14_168. The divisional commander (centre) pictured during a visit to a gun pit of 1.Battery Reserve Feldartillerie Regiment 26, during July 1916.

ATT_14_169/a. (Left) The Town Hall in Miraumont during the Somme battle. (Above) Another view of the damage caused in Miraumont by British shelling.

ATT_14_170/170a. Originally captioned 'Sanitary dump near Miraumont', this shows a woodland hollow in use as a casualty clearing station during the Somme fighting between July and October 1916. (Right) A staff car approaching Miraumont after the start of the battle. On the left is a concrete shelter which is unaffected by the shelling.

ATT_14_171/171a. (Left) Another view of the Casualty Clearing Station at Miraumont. (Below) A staff car driving past the Town Hall shortly after the start of the Somme battle.

ATT_14_172. British soldiers captured on 1 July.

ATT_14_174. The commander of 2.Armee during the Somme battles, General Fritz von Below, pictured here leaving 26 Reserve Infantry Division's Headquarters.

ATT_14_173. Erroneously captioned as 'Australian PoWs at Divisional Staff Quarters in Biefvillers during July', these men are not wearing Australian tunics and are British soldiers.

ATT_14_175. A Field Church Service during the Somme battle.

ATT_14_176. Pictured standing in the positions of Reserve Infantry Regiment 121 at Serre is the Regimental Commander Oberst Josenhans. He died in 1919 as a result of his war service.

ATT_14_177. A bivouac area in the village of Biefvillers.

ATT_14_178. The Württemberg field hospital was in the château in Vélu.

ATT_14_179. Havrincourt Château was used by the division as a convalescent home.

ATT_14_180. The Serre Calvary taken in August 1916.

ATT_14_181. How the Calvary had appeared to troops stationed in Serre in May.

ATT_14_183. The 'Funf Weiden' (five willows) area in August, a few months after photo 143 was taken.

ATT_14_182. A building in Serre known as the Cloister.

ATT_14_184. Hauptmann Maul of Reserve Infantry Regiment 119 was killed during the Somme fighting.

ATT_14_185. The Leiling position (see photo 67) south of Beaumont in August 1916.

ATT_14_186. The Ancre Valley in August 1916. The narrow gauge rail line was the target and the trees are collateral damage.

ATT_14_187. As in the British Army, when there was no obvious use for the cavalry, they were used in the line. These are Württembergisches Reserve-Dragoons in the trench at Beaucourt during the battle.

ATT_14_188. A view from the front positions, south of Saint-Pierre Divion. On the right, German positions and on the left the British positions north of the Ancre.

ATT_14_192. A narrow gauge railway was used to bring materials to the Pioneer Park at Irles. The huge quantities of timber needed to make the trenches secure are clearly seen.

ATT_14_190. A minenwerfer about to be fired during the Somme battle.

ATT_14_189. The main road through Grandcourt during the Somme battle.

ATT_14_191. Reserve troops in the Ancre valley, west of Miraumont, during the British offensive on the Somme.

ATT_14_194. Damage to the church tower in Grévillers was caused, according to the caption, by naval guns.

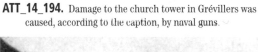

ATT_14_193. Major Majer, 1.Battalion Infantry Regiment 180, was killed in the fighting for Thiepval during September 1916.

ATT_14_196. The grain harvest near Bapaume during the Somme battle.

ATT_14_195. Another view of Grévillers after the bombardment.

ATT_14_197. Wagons of the ammunition column of Reserve Field Artillery Regiment 26 near Favreuil, after being bombed by British aircraft.

ATT_14_198. A British biplane shot down in July 1916 is being inspected by staff officers. The captured pilot is standing in the centre of the picture.

ATT_14_199. Reserve troops at Miraumont during the Somme battle, waiting to be called to the front.

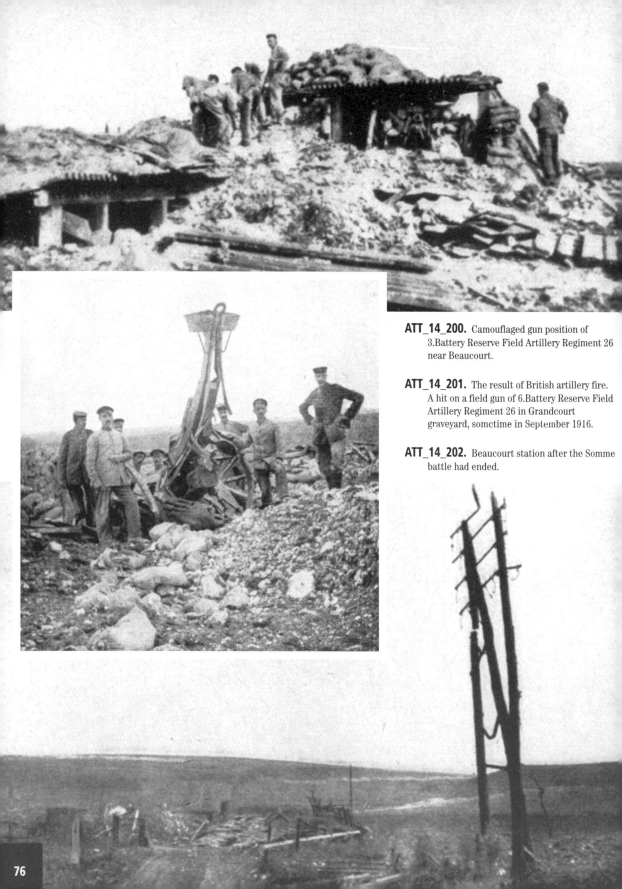

ATT_14_200. Camouflaged gun position of 3.Battery Reserve Field Artillery Regiment 26 near Beaucourt.

ATT_14_201. The result of British artillery fire. A hit on a field gun of 6.Battery Reserve Field Artillery Regiment 26 in Grandcourt graveyard, somctime in September 1916.

ATT_14_202. Beaucourt station after the Somme battle had ended.

ATT_14_203. Dead British soldiers in the front trenches of the Beaumont-south sector on the evening of 3 September.

ATT_14_204. The crater made by a heavy British shell that exploded just behind a gun position of 6.Battery Reserve Field Artillery Regiment 26 in October 1916, near Miraumont.

ATT_14_205/205a.

(Above) The result of a direct hit on a gun of 6.Batterie Reserve Field Artillery Regiment 26 from British counter-battery fire during the Somme battle. (Right) Three British soldiers and some of the weapons captured during the fighting on 3 September 1916, near Beaumont.

ATT_14_206/206a. (Above) Counter-attack troops resting whilst waiting for orders. (Left) A trench in Thiepval – a 38cm British shell that failed to explode.

ATT_14_208. Courcelette in September 1916.

ATT_14_207/207a/207b. (Above) A patrol called 'British Death' photographed before it left for operations in Thiepval Forest on 7 September 1916. (Left) By September 1916 most of the trees in Thiepval Park showed considerable damage. (Below) Thiepval Park in July 1916, showing the damage caused by British shelling.

ATT_14_209. The commander of 52 Reserve Infantry Brigade 52, Generalleutnant von Auwärter, in front of his headquarters.

ATT_14_210. After a successful defence of the cornerstone of the Somme battle, Thiepval, detached combat troops of Infantry Regiment 180 in Achiet-le-Grand in September 1916.

ATT_14_211. A photo taken in Miraumont at the beginning of October 1916.

ATT_14_212. Villages in rear areas looked the same after months of fighting. This is Vaulx-Vraucourt in October 1916. The church pictured was used a billet by the troops.

ATT_14_213. Combat-ready troops resting in the church at Vaulx-Vraucourt in October 1916.

ATT_14_214. A distant view of another unaffected village – Croisilles in October 1916.

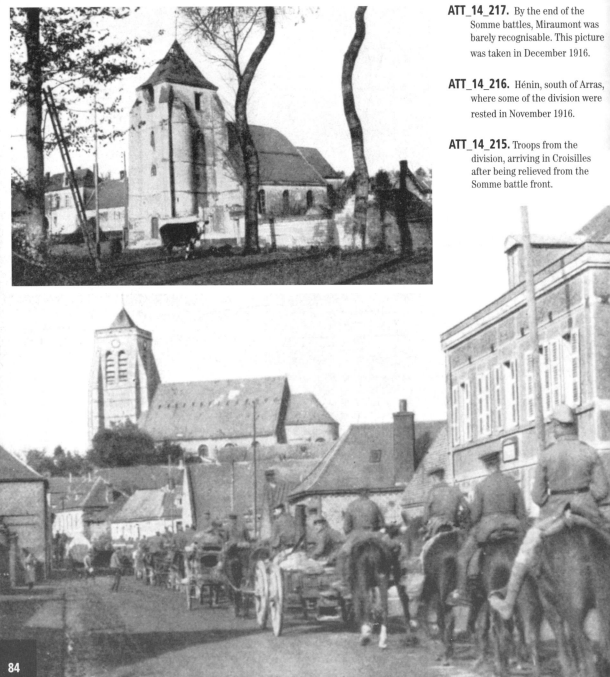

ATT_14_217. By the end of the Somme battles, Miraumont was barely recognisable. This picture was taken in December 1916.

ATT_14_216. Hénin, south of Arras, where some of the division were rested in November 1916.

ATT_14_215. Troops from the division, arriving in Croisilles after being relieved from the Somme battle front.

ATT_14_218. The main street through the village of Ransart in late 1916.

ATT_14_220. The military cemetery in Ransart, complete with stone memorial, during the winter of 1916/17.

ATT_14_219. A typical French roadside scene – a Calvary at a fork in the road Boiry – Hendecourt and Boiry – Boisleux.

ATT_14_221/221a/221b. (Above) Officers discussing positions after their arrival in Monchy-au-Bois at the end of 1916. (Left) Hamelincourt Château in 1916. (Below) Drawing fresh water from a typical Northern French well in Hamelincourt.

ATT_14_222/222a. (Above) An Allied aircraft shot down near Adinfer in November 1916. (Left) Boelcke's 37th victim fell to earth between Bullecourt and Croisilles on 22 October. The burning plane is a Sopwith 1½ Strutter. Oscar Boelke was killed only days later, on 28 October.

ATT_14_223. The divisional staff pose together on the departure of their Commanding Officer, General von Soden.

ATT_14_224a. A British aircraft shot down near Favreuil by a German Albatross single-seat fighter.

Part Two
From the beginning of 1917
to the end of the war

During 1917 the division spent time in France and Belgium and was involved in numerous battles, ending back where it began in 1914. As well as losing its commanding officer, the division was also reduced in size when it gave up Reserve Infantry Regiment 99 to newly formed 220 Division. The division now comprised one brigade of three infantry regiments under Oberst Walther and six artillery batteries under Oberstleutnant von Lewinski and was completely composed of men from Württemberg.

I. The withdrawal to, and the fighting in, the Siegfried Line
January to August 1917

January and February 1917 found the division in the quiet sector of Croisilles. During this period they made preparations for Operation Alberich and their withdrawal to the Siegfried Line and its prepared positions. This had been ordered by OHL in order to shorten the line. The withdrawal was subject to heavy pressure from British activity but the bulk of the forces arrived intact, often after brave rearguard actions.

Shortly after taking up positions, the division was moved on 10 April to the Valenciennes area. The intention was that here it should be rested and trained for its future role. The rest was short-lived because the British had begun their attack in the Arras region on 9 April. Reserve Infantry Regiment 121 was soon in action near Vis-en-Artois and the remainder of the division was sent to north-east of Saint-Quentin. Initially intended as a counter-attack division, it became a line-holding division in the southern sector of Saint-Quentin – Neuville-Saint-Amand.

As a result of the continued British attacks, it moved back to the Arras area, for a brief period, as an *Eingreifdivision* (counter-attack division). It then returned to the front as a line-holding division and fought in the Bullecourt – Quéant position. As well as fighting and patrol work, much time was spent on repairing the line before handing over to a replacement division when the division moved to Flanders.

II. The Battle of Ypres and the trench warfare in Flanders
August 1917 to February 1918

As a result of the British offensive in Flanders, the division was sent to Kortrijk. A few days after arrival, it was moved to Torhout and Staden before being thrown into battle near Broenbach, between Papegoed and Langemarck, on 19 August. The crater-filled battlefield, offering little protection from the elements, artillery fire or aircraft, pushed the men to their limits, especially as they were constantly at combat readiness. However, this did not stop them successfully defending their sector. Reserve Infantry Regiment 121 was particularly effective in the fighting in the Totenwaldchen (Dead Copse) area where it captured many prisoners and much equipment.

On 18 September, part of the division was transported via Lille to Saint-Quentin where it was to be rested and trained. However, after three weeks, it was sent back to Flanders – destination Lichtervelde. The division now found itself on the southern edge of Houthulst Forest where the fighting was especially heavy, communication very difficult and casualties high. After fighting in the sector from 17 to 23 October it was rested, becoming a reserve division in the Eerneghem area.

In early November, the division was relieved and marched north to a quieter sector on the Yser Canal in the area of Schoorbakke – Beerst (north of Diksmuide). This was a flooded area where there was little activity and the division was able to rest and recover.

Shortly before Christmas, the rest came to an end when the division returned to the sector between Blankaartsee and the northern edge of Houthulst Forest. Once again, in inadequate shelters and against a very active enemy, the division suffered considerably.

Just before the German offensive in March, Allied intelligence reported that it was a very good division – the men would have agreed with that – it had stubbornly resisted British attacks on the Somme and launched vigorous counter-attacks. As it had not been seriously engaged since then – although the men of the division would have disagreed with this statement – they were thoroughly rested as the division had not been exposed to the violent Flanders battles, nor suffered great losses; as a result its morale had not been shaken.

III. The Spring offensive in Artois
March to June 1918

In mid-February the division was taken from the front-line and sent to guard the

Belgian–Dutch border. However, while it was engaged in border patrols, it trained for the forthcoming offensive as an 'Attack Division'. After a five-day rest near Tournai it began the march to its positions for the March Offensive. Marching only at night to prevent observation by Allied aircraft, by 19 March the infantry reached its assembly area: Lécluse – Éterpigny –Vis-en-Artois, and found the artillery already in position. Its mission was to protect the troops engaged in the main attack further to the south against a flanking movement by the British troops massed around Arras.

The division, initially in reserve behind the attack on Bapaume – Peronne, waited over a day for the call *'Vorwarts'*. The first unit to move was Reserve Infantry Regiment 119 which quickly took Croisilles Heights and, on 23 March, Héninel.

St. Martin-sur-Cojeul and Hénin-sur-Cojeul were stormed by Reserve Infantry Regiment 121 and Infantry Regiment 180 on 25 March. Further progress was hampered by the shell-cratered battlefield that made it difficult for the artillery and ammunition columns to be brought forward. It was not until 28 March that the advance continued and the division managed to push through enemy trenches, taking more than 300 prisoners and much booty.

OIL closed down further attacks in the Arras sector and ordered the division to dig-in on the captured positions between Neuville – Becquerelle – Boiry. This task was made more difficult by heavy rain and heavy enemy artillery fire against which the troops had little defence.

After nearly two months of almost continual fighting, the division was reported to have lost sixty per cent of its strength. As a result of its losses, it was replaced in mid-May and sent to the Bugnicourt – Arleux – Écourt area for rest, reinforcement and training.

IV. Defensive battles in northern France on both sides of the road Cambrai – Arras and the Battle of Cambrai
June to November 1918

After the rest, the division expected to be used once again as an 'Attack Division', but instead, with the continued Allied pressure, it took the defensive. From Arleux it marched to the battlefields in which it had fought during 1915/16 to relieve 41st Division on 9 June. The area they had left had become a desert of rubble; the positions they had built were unrecognisable. Their new positions were very close to the enemy and required constant vigilance, but readiness to combat any attack was severely hampered by the flu, which meant that many squads were at a tenth of their combat strength. A week later, the division extended its front southwards to relieve 16th Reserve Division. Even so, when the British resumed large scale attacks in mid-July, causing severe losses, the division was able to hold its positions for a full ten days before being relieved by the 183rd Division.

After relief the division was sent to Ytres to rest in 'extremely primitive accommodation in corrugated iron huts' captured from the British. The heavy fighting had adversely impacted on the men's mental condition and the rest did little to improve this. As a result they were sent to Douai for further rest.

While Reserve Infantry Regiment 119 was filmed marching north, part of the artillery continued to fight in the Bray – Cappy area. Although the division was in Douai to rest, it was attached to I.Bavarian Reserve Korps as a counter-attack division. This, with the constant moving of camp, and having to hold the second line between Beaumont and Brebières, meant that in reality there was little time for resting. With an increase in British activity on the Scarpe, the division was moved back to the Chérisy – Vis-en-Artois sector. During this period, the size of a battalion fell from four to three companies due to the shortage of replacements across the whole army.

A major Allied attack on 27 August on the Arras – Cambrai sector broke through the front but 26th Reserve Division held its lines against the superior force of English and Canadian troops while again suffering heavy losses. Divisions on either side did not fare as well and 26th Divisional Command assumed control of their units. In total the division now controlled eleven infantry regiments, five field and six heavy artillery regiments.

After four days of almost continuous fighting, the division was exhausted but, as usual, was able to hand over to its replacement division the positions they held at the start of the attack. Rest consisted of a march to the Scarpe Canal in Douai, on to positions held by IV.Armee Korps in Seclin and finally to their destination, XXXX.Reserve Armee Korps around Lens. In the twenty-six days following the start of the British offensive, the division moved eleven times across four army fronts and was called upon to fight whenever the situation required.

On 20 September, in Thumieres, north of Douai, the Division was honoured to be greeted by Field Marshal von Hindenburg.

As a result of the progress of the British attacks along the road between Arras – Cambrai, the division was moved back, on 22 September, to Bouchain to help counter an anticipated major English (sic) attack south of Cambrai behind the right wing of 2.Armee at Beauvois. Between 28 September and 2 October, the division distinguished itself in action between Blécourt and Ramillies, defending its positions against superior numbers of troops supported by tanks. As a result, the division was able to withdraw with its artillery and after twelve days was replaced in the line. During this fighting it was heavily engaged and fought very well, according to Allied intelligence. They rated it as a first-class division that had distinguished itself during the Cambrai action. It was always dependable and on the whole fought well.

This is corroborated by the action of General von Below, commander of 17.Armee, in which they were serving. He 'sent a telegram to the King. . . saying that the division had fought in an exemplary manner at Cambrai, where it had several times re-established the situation by its counter-attacks on the 29th, inflicting enormous losses on the enemy, and thus preventing the town from falling into their hands.'

Even though the division was headed north it was temporarily pulled in to assist in the defence of Douai before moving to the Hermann positions on the Scheldt Canal. Here it beat off several enemy attacks and it was still in the line on 11 November.

In recognition of the accounts of the division's service in army reports during the withdrawal, the divisional commander was awarded the Pour le Mérite.

V. Retreat and return
November to December 1918

With the changing political situation the division moved independently to the south-west of Brussels. By 10 November the division had reformed and was ready to defend the Meuse positions, but the position at home and the Armistice made this unnecessary.

Immediately after the Armistice the division prepared for the march home. With flags flying, the division joined other units on 14 November, in a highly disciplined march home, proud to have done their duty with 'spotless honour'. The division arrived back in Württemberg in early December and was disbanded.

The division's historians felt that they had 'endured the roaring storm' and that future generations should, from this history, draw inspiration from this record of German power, toughness and endurance, while recalling that all this must be based on discipline, sense of duty and camaraderie.

ATT_14_225. Moyenneville, south of Arras in December 1916, where the division was sent to rest after the Somme battles.

ATT_14_224. Generalleutnant z. D. Albert Hermann von Fritsch took over command of the division on 17 December 1916.

ATT_14_226. Men of Reserve Infantry Regiment 121 standing in the centre of Ayette in December 1916.

ATT_14_227/227a. (Above) Douchy-lès-Ayette, where Infantry Regiment 180 was quartered. (Below) Christmas 1916 – men of Reserve Infantry Regiment 119 celebrating in the forward position of the Blaireville sector.

ATT_14_228. Adinfer was another relatively unscathed village.

ATT_14_229. Monchy-au-Bois was in the sector held by Infantry Regiment 180 during the winter of 1916/17.

ATT_14_230. Grande Ferme du Bois du Quesnoy.

ATT_14_231/231a. (Above) Troops from the division celebrating the Kaiser's birthday on 27 January 1917, in Croisilles. (Below) The divisional train leaving Croisilles in February 1917, during the withdrawal to the Siegfried Line.

ATT_14_232. Clearing up in Croisilles before the withdrawal to the Siegfried positions in March 1917. The soldier is taking a cow with him on the march.

ATT_14_233. Civilians loading their possessions on to wagons before they were evacuated ahead of the withdrawal.

ATT_14_234. Croisilles during the withdrawal in March 1917.

ATT_14_235. Another view of Croisilles in March.

ATT_14_236. During the withdrawal the division passed through Saudemont, north west of Cambrai.

J. Saudemont

ATT_14_237. Another village they passed through on their way to Saint-Quentin was Écourt-Saint-Quentin.

ATT_14_238. British prisoners with their captors in Villers-lès-Cagnicourt in March 1917. They had been captured during an attack on British forward posts near Écoust-Saint-Mein.

ATT_14_239.

British troops captured in the outpost fighting around Écoust-Saint-Mein and Noreuil in March 1917.

ATT_14_241. Séboncourt in the middle of April 1917. During this period the division was the *Eingrief* (immediate counter-attack) division for the Saint-Quentin sector.

ATT_14_240. Valenciennes Market Square and Town Hall. Part of the division was here in April 1917.

ATT_14_242. A view of Origny, an undamaged village, showing the road to Saint-Quentin.

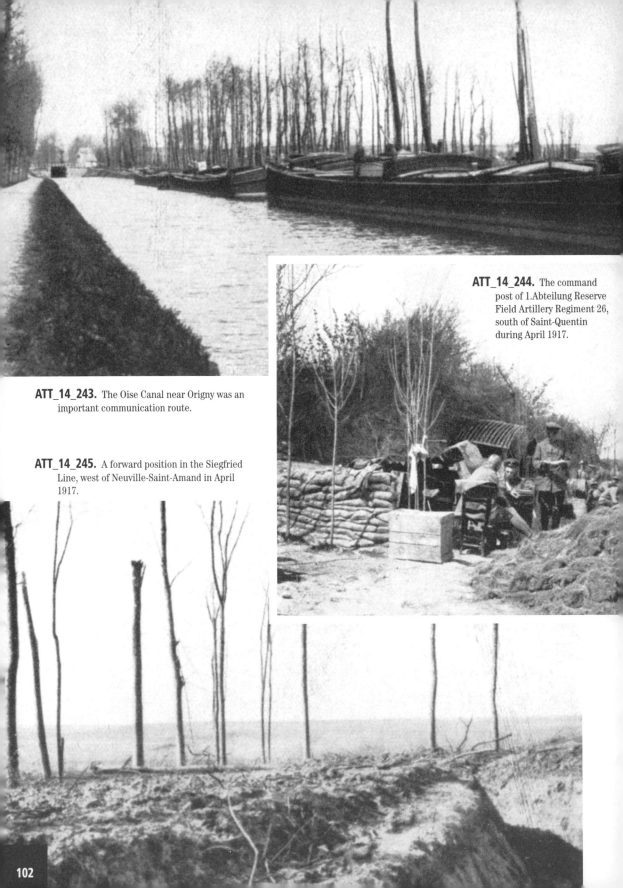

ATT_14_243. The Oise Canal near Origny was an important communication route.

ATT_14_244. The command post of 1.Abteilung Reserve Field Artillery Regiment 26, south of Saint-Quentin during April 1917.

ATT_14_245. A forward position in the Siegfried Line, west of Neuville-Saint-Amand in April 1917.

ATT_14_246. A field gun position hidden in a garden on the outskirts of Saint-Quentin in April 1917.

ATT_14_248. The cathedral interior shows clear signs of misuse.

ATT_14_247. The cathedral of Saint-Quentin showed no obvious signs of damage in April 1917.

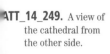

ATT_14_249. A view of the cathedral from the other side.

ATT_14_250. The Town Hall in Saint-Quentin in April 1917. A once busy thoroughfare is deserted.

ATT_14_251. Another unspoiled town: Oisy-le-Verger, north west of Cambrai in April 1917.

ATT_14_252. The village of Sauchy-Lestrée, north west of Cambrai.

ATT_14_253. The official stopping place for vehicles on the move from Villers-lès-Cagnicourt to Cagnicourt, taken sometime between May and July 1917.

ATT_14_254. A German soldier riding through Cagnicourt, a town showing damage from the 1914 fighting.

ATT_14_255/255a. (Left) Hendecourt Château after the fighting in the area between May and August 1917. (Below) Trench shelters for counter-attack troops on the southern edge of Hendecourt.

ATT_14_256. Hendecourt, 4km behind the Siegfried positions, was completely destroyed within a few days of the commencement of the English barrage in April 1917.

ATT_14_257. A counter-attack company waiting in Hendecourt.

ATT_14_258. The 'Raperie', the remains of a sugar beet factory, on the road from Bullecourt to Hendecourt in May 1917.

ATT_14_259. Looking out at Bullecourt from the front trench – a shell crater – in June 1917.

ATT_14_261. The Bullecourt battlefield from 3,000 metres.

ATT_14_261. A forward position at Bullecourt – in reality a shell hole.

ATT_14_260. A lookout can be seen surveying 'Raven Valley' from the security of his position in the remains of a large mill north west of Bullecourt.

ATT_14_263. The combat area to the west of Bullecourt from 1800m – Écoust-Saint-Mein is in the centre of the view.

Écoust St Mein

ATT_14_265. Riencourt in June 1917.

ATT_14_264. The 'Fighting Troops' commander on the road between Hendecourt and Riencourt sometime between May and July 1917. Note the debris and the dugouts along the road.

ATT_14_266. Immediately in front of the Hindenburg Line, a British tank that was destroyed by artillery fire.

ATT_14_268. Sauchicourt Farm, near Sauchy-Lestrée, was the staff headquarters of Reserve Infantry Brigade 51.

ATT_14_267. Bathing in the Sensée lakes somewhere near Croisilles.

ATT_14_269. The countryside around the Sensée lakes in July 1917.

ATT_14_270. The division marching through Kortrijk in Belgium on their way to Ypres.

ATT_14_272. After Kortrijk, the division moved to Harlebeke and then Torhout.

ATT_14_271. Relatively untouched by the war, Kortrijk in August 1917, was a busy town.

ATT_14_274. A view of Torhout, in August, showing the division marching through to their concentration area before leaving for the trenches.

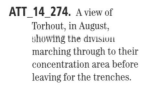

ATT_14_273. Not all the division had marched from France, some arrived by train. Here they are shown arriving at Torhout station in August 1917.

ATT_14_275. Another view of the undamaged town of Torhout.

ATT_14_276. Marching to the front in Flanders. This is the small town of Gits in August 1917.

ATT_14_278. Infantry marching through Sint Jozef after leaving Staden.

ATT_14_277. From Gits, the division marched through Staden in a northerly direction.

ATT_14_280. The château in Houthulst Forest during August/September 1917.

ATT_14_279. On arrival at Ondank, near the front, the division set up in shelters on the eastern edge of Houthulst Forest.

ATT_14_281. The 'counter-attack troops' headquarters at Papegoed farm near Bixschoote in August 1917.

ATT_14_282. Concrete headquarters post near the Broen Brook between Langemarck and Poelkapelle.

ATT_14_283. The peaceful town of Bohain near Saint-Quentin in October 1917.

ATT_14_285/285a, Lichtervelde in October 1917. The house is still standing but the area around it is heavily built up. (Left) Some of the damage caused by the British bombing of Lichtervelde in October 1917.

ATT_14_284. A forward position in a large shell crater in 'Totenwäldchen' near Broen Brook.

ATT_14_286/286a. British troops captured during the advance of Reserve Infantry Regiment 121 in 'Totenwäldchen'.

ATT_14_287. 'English kindness for the residents of Lichtervelde': the results of a British bombardment.

ATT_14_288. Catching a nap in 'Totenwäldchen' sometime in October 1917.

ATT_14_290. A closer view of the cathedral in Saint-Quentin.

ATT_14_289. The market square and cathedral in Saint-Quentin in October 1917.

ATT_14_291. The château at White House in Houthulst Forest.

ATT_14_292. Inside Saint-Quentin Cathedral in October 1917.

ATT_14_293. Friedrich Street in Houthulst Forest in October 1917, complete with dead horse. Note there is little left of the forest.

ATT_14_294. Kortemarck, behind the lines, in October 1917.

ATT_14_295. German positions in Houthulst Forest viewed from the air.

ATT_14_296. Counter-attack troops, in their temporary accommodation in the church at Gits, sometime in October 1917, during a rest period.

ATT_14_297. The divisional headquarters was based in a convent in Gits during October and November.

ATT_14_299/299a.
A view of the Yser positions in November 1917.

ATT_14_298. With positions on both sides of the Yser Canal in November, it was necessary to maintain water transport in case the footbridge was destroyed by British artillery fire.

ATT_14_300. The remains of the church at Jonkershove on the north side of Houthulst Forest.

ATT_14_301. Shelters in Keiem, a small town near Diksmuide.

ATT_14_302. The shell-marked terrain near Beerst, north of Diksmuide.

ATT_14_303. A footbridge, near Stuivenkerke, north of Diksmuide, over the land flooded by the Belgians to stop the German advance.

ATT_14_304. The divisional baggage column in the town square at Eernegem, north west of Torhout, during the winter of 1917/18. Eernegem was the divisional staff headquarters.

ATT_14_305. Bruges, where men from the division were sent on leave.

ATT_14_308. A street in Handzame, east of Diksmuide.

ATT_14_309. The church in Werken, east of Diksmuide.

ATT_14_306. Ostend, another destination for men on leave, during the winter of 1917/18.

ATT_14_307. Ostend was an important naval base. This is a torpedo boat in the harbour between patrols.

ATT_14_310. Blankaart Lake Château in December 1917.

ATT_14_311. A view of the battlefield near Blankaart Lake in December 1917.

ATT_14_312. A view across Blankaart Lake in December 1917.

ATT_14_314. Concrete shelters near Blankaart Lake Château.

ATT_14_315. Concrete shelters near Blankaart Lake.

ATT_14_313. Constructing concrete shelters near Jonkershove, to the north of Houthulst Forest.

ATT_14_316. The church tower in Zarren, showing earlier damage.

ATT_14_317. Wynendaele Château near Torhout in the winter of 1917/1918.

ATT_14_318/318a. (Left) Divisional staff transport in Lokeren in March 1918 as they were about to leave for France. (Below) Behind the lines, Lokeren, pictured in the middle of March 1918, was used as a rest area for troops on the Flanders front.

ATT_14_320/320a. (Left) Bridge over the Schelde between Tournai and Antoing. (Right) One of many photos taken during the move to France in March 1918 was this view of the Schelde Canal south east of Tournai.

ATT_14_319. Lokeren town centre in early 1918.

ATT_14_321. Temporary marching headquarters in Rosult during the move to their positions in France for the March offensive.

ATT_14_322. Combat baggage being loaded during the move to France.

ATT_14_323. The Signals Section of Infantry Regiment 180 resting during the march to France.

ATT_14_324. A country house in Lallaing seen during the march to France.

ATT_14_325. The division arrived in Vis-en-Artois during March in readiness for its part in the forthcoming offensive.

ATT_14_327. Divisional heavy battery setting up its firing positions shortly after arriving on their allotted sector.

ATT_14_329. 26th Reserve Division troops in their
assembly positions on 22 March waiting for zero hour.

ATT_14_326. Company commanders drawing up orders for
the attack on 21 March.

ATT_14_328. 9.Battery, Reserve Field Artillery Regiment 26 near Vis-en-Artois, firing against British positions on
21 March, 1918.

ATT_14_330. Infantry accompanying a field gun over the cratered battlefield during the attempt to take Croisilles Heights and Héninel on 23 March, 1918.

ATT_14_331. Captured British position, the firing line of the second system according to the notice board, near Chérisy on 22 March, 1918.

ATT_14_332. The Divisional Commander with some of the counter-attack troops in a newly reconquered section of the Siegfried Line.

ATT_14_334. The badly damaged town of Héninel seen on 23 March, 1918.

ATT_14_333. A Signal Lamp detachment in position on Croisilles Heights.

ATT_14_336. A light field gun in action on Croisilles Heights.

ATT_14_338. The Cojeul brook near Hénin after the March fighting.

ATT_14_337. Tracked vehicles were often used to carry ammunition to battery positions in March and April 1918.

ATT_14_339. The command post of Infantry Regiment 180 was in a captured British artillery position near Hénin.

ATT_14_340. British troops captured during the fighting around Croisilles Heights and in the Cojeul valley, sometime in March 1918.

ATT_14_342. A British field gun captured during the March attacks.

ATT_14_341. A mobile radio transmitter in use during the offensive. Note the long aerial and electric motor to provide power.

ATT_14_343. The division set up its command post during the March advance in a chalk pit near Fontaine.

ATT_14_344. The divisional baggage train preparing for an overnight stop near Chérisy during the advance.

ATT_14_345. The divisional train moving through Chérisy during March 1918.

ATT_14_346. Another view of the divisional train passing through Chérisy.

ATT_14_347. The divisional commander during a visit to a newly set-up heavy battery.

ATT_14_348. The divisional commander near Chérisy in March with four unknown men, three of whom appear to be more interested in the photographer than what their general is talking about.

ATT_14_349. German troops inspecting British weapons captured during the recent fighting.

ATT_14_350. Fighting troops moving through the newly captured town of Croisilles on 25 March 1918.

ATT_14_351. Newly captured British soldiers, nearly all of whom are looking at the camera for the picture.

ATT_14_352. The senior General Staff officer of the division reading papers in a temporary HQ during the advance.

ATT_14_353. By the end of April the division was near Cambrai. This building in Lécluse was used as its temporary headquarters.

ATT_14_354. A captured British camp near Écoust-Saint-Mein was put to use by the division.

ATT_14_355. The British camp near Mory was also put to further use after its capture.

ATT_14_356. A wayside dump near Estrée. Materiel was brought up by narrow gauge trains.

ATT_14_357/357a/357b. (Above) Unloading provisions at Espérance Farm near Dury on the road between Arras and Cambrai. Photos 357a and 357b show Divisional shelters between Dury and Hendecourt in August 1918.

ATT_14_358. A divisional heavy artillery battery resting after being temporarily detached from their regiment.

ATT_14_359. Écourt-Saint-Quentin during the offensive, appearing to be a quiet town and showing little material damage.

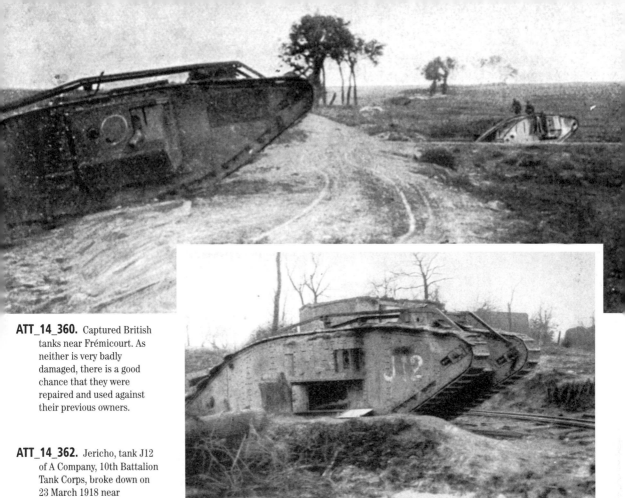

ATT_14_360. Captured British tanks near Frémicourt. As neither is very badly damaged, there is a good chance that they were repaired and used against their previous owners.

ATT_14_362. Jericho, tank J12 of A Company, 10th Battalion Tank Corps, broke down on 23 March 1918 near Bapaume. It was still there in July when this photograph was taken.

ATT_14_361. A British artillery dump captured, complete with narrow gauge rail track, on the road between Bapaume and Béugny.

ATT_14_364. All that remained of the memorial to General Faidherbe was the plinth. The area around it had also suffered severe damage. Compare with photo on page 31.

ATT_14_363. A view of the ruins of Bapaume in July 1918.

ATT_14_365. Captured English Nissen huts on the road between Biefvillers and Bihucourt.

ATT_14_366. A divisional camp on the outskirts of Bapaume in July 1918.

ATT_14_367. A Biefvillers country house in July 1918.

ATT_14_368. A small lake just off the main road from Biefvillers to Biłucourt showing shell damage to trees and buildings.

ATT_14_370. The division used a British Nissen Hut in Grévillers as its operations headquarters during July 1918.

ATT_14_369. The divisional commander's quarters in Grévillers in July, complete with sandbag protection and a guard.

ATT_14_371. The division's weather section at work during June 1918. They are about to release a balloon to check wind movements.

ATT_14_372. The Casualty Clearing Station at Irles in July 1918.

ATT_14_373. Even though there is a Red Cross flag on the roof of the Nissen Hut, in use as a Casualty Clearing Station at Irles, it shows damage. The original caption states that it was bombed by English bombers.

ATT_14_374. A makeshift bakery in the newly reoccupied territory on the Somme during June/July 1918.

ATT_14_375. A railway bridge in Miraumont destroyed by the British during the withdrawal on the Somme Front.

ATT_14_376. Miraumont in July 1918. Little is left standing.

ATT_14_377. Miraumont as the advancing German Army found it in 1918.

ATT_14_378. The church, memorial and military cemetery after the British had retreated from Miraumont.

ATT_14_379. Shelling during the offensive destroyed the military cemetery and damaged the memorial to the dead of 26th Reserve Infantry Division. The damage was blamed on the 'English' in the original caption but could have been caused by both sides.

ATT_14_380. This Miraumont building photographed, taken in July 1918, was the Divisional Staff Quarters during 1914/15. In the foreground is a heavy field artillery piece.

ATT_14_381. The road from Miraumont to Puisieux, taken in July 1918 facing Puisieux.

ATT_14_382. How 26th Reserve Division found the 1915/16 Soldiers' Cemetery when they returned in 1918.

ATT_14_383. Another view of the damage to the 1915/16 cemetery.

ATT_14_384. The road from Puisieux to Beaucourt, looking towards Beaucourt, in 1918.

ATT_14_385. The Butte de Warlencourt seen in July 1918.

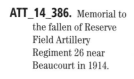

ATT_14_386. Memorial to the fallen of Reserve Field Artillery Regiment 26 near Beaucourt in 1914.

ATT_14_387. On their return in 1918, the gunners found that their memorial had been badly hit by shells during the fighting.

ATT_14_388. Warlencourt in August 1918.

ATT_14_389. A British ammunition train hit by German bombers near Courcelette in 1918.

ATT_14_390. Courcelette in 1918 seen from the Pozières road exit.

ATT_14_391. Albert in 1918 after the Golden Virgin had fallen.

ATT_14_392. The Basilica of Notre-Dame de Brebières in Albert after the British had withdrawn.

ATT_14_393. The division was rested in August 1918 in a camp known as WeserLager at Ytres. This is the divisional commander's personal accommodation.

ATT_14_394. The divisional staff did not warrant a solid building but were camped in captured British tents.

ATT_14_396. This bridge over the canal near Ytres was destroyed by the British during their withdrawal.

ATT_14_395. During the defensive fighting on the Somme in August 1918, Infantry Regiment 180 and 1.Detachment Reserve Field Artillery Regiment 26, were stationed at Cappy.

ATT_14_399. A camouflaged anti-tank gun near Vis-en Artois at the end of August, during the defensive fighting against the British offensive.

ATT_14_397/397a. (Above) A view of the village of Cappy near Bray-sur-Somme. (Left) Douai, when the division withdrew through the city, was an empty place. This is the Beffroi de Douai in the city centre.

ATT_14_398. Château Goeulzin, south of Douai, pictured in August/September 1918, during the division's withdrawal to the Schelde defences.

ATT_14_400. Generalfeldmarschall von Hindenburg inspected the division while it was stationed in Thumeries, north of Douai, in September 1918.

ATT_14_402. The canal through Douai, now a forward position, at the end of September.

ATT_14_401. The artillery units also helped provide defence against aircraft attacks. A machine gun is mounted on a rotating plinth to allow it to shoot upwards and in all directions without having to change its position.

ATT_14_404. Another view of Saint-Amand as the division passed through in November.

ATT_14_403. The division passed through Saint-Amand during its withdrawal to the Schelde positions.

ATT_14_405. By December the division was back in Germany. This picture is simply captioned 'Homecoming – December 1918'.

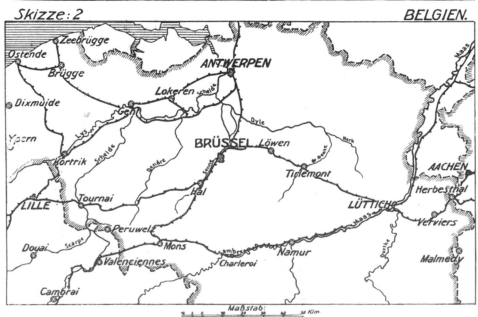

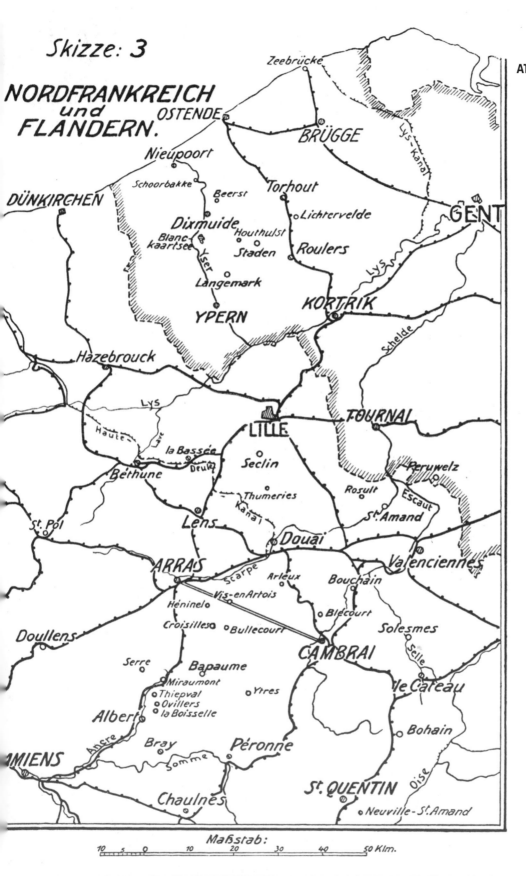

Skizze: 3

NORDFRANKREICH und FLANDERN.

Zeebrücke
OSTENDE
BRÜGGE
GENT
Nieupoort
DÜNKIRCHEN
Schoorbakke
Beerst
Torhout
Lichtervelde
Dixmuide
Houthulst
Lys-Kanal
Blanc-kaartsee
Yser
Staden
Roulers
Langemark
YPERN
KORTRIK
Lys
Hazebrouck
Schelde
Lys
TOURNAI
Haute
LILLE
Peruwelz
la Bassée
Seclin
Escaut
Béthune
Deulr
Thumeries
Rosult
St. Pol
Kanal
St. Amand
Lens
Douai
Valenciennes
ARRAS
Scarpe
Arleux
Bouchain
Vis-enArtois
Héninel
Blécourt
Doullens
Croisilles
Bullecourt
Solesmes
Serre
Bapaume
CAMBRAI
Selle
Miraumont
le Cateau
Thiepval
Ytres
Ovillers
la Boisselle
Albert
Bohain
Ancre
Bray
Péronne
AMIENS
Somme
St. QUENTIN
Chaulnes
Oise
Neuville-St. Amand

Maßstab:
10 5 0   10   20   30   40   50 Klm.

26. (Württembergische)
Reserve-Division 1914-1918

Order of battle 2 August 1914

51. Reserve-Infanterie-Brigade
10. Württembergisches Inf. Regiment Nr. 180
Reserve-Inf. Regiment Nr. 121

52. Reserve-Infanterie-Brigade
Reserve-Inf. Regiment Nr. 119
Reserve-Inf. Regiment Nr. 120
Württembergisches Reserve-Dragoner-Regiment
Reserve-Feldartillerie-Regiment Nr. 26
4. Kompagnie Pionier-Bataillon Nr. 13

Order of battle 20 March 1918

51. Reserve-Infanterie-Brigade
Reserve-Inf.Regiment Nr. 119
Reserve-Inf. Regiment Nr. 121
10. Württembergisches Inf. Regiment Nr. 180
Maschinen-Gewehr-Scharfschützen-Abteilung 54
2. Eskadron Ulanen-Regiment Nr. 20

Artillerie-Kommandeur 122
Reserve-Feldartillerie-Regiment Nr. 26
Fußartillerie-Bataillon 59

Stab Pionier-Bataillon 326
4. Kompagnie Pionier-Bataillon Nr. 13
6. Kompagnie Pionier-Bataillon Nr. 13
Minenwerfer-Kompagnie 226

Divisions-Nachrichten-Kommandeur 426

Commanders

26. (Württembergische) Reserve-Division 1914-1918

02.08.1914-17.12.1916 General der Infanterie z. D. Franz Freiherr von Soden
17.12.1916-Ende Generalleutnant z. D. Albert Hermann von Fritsch

Losses

Killed: 446 officers, 13,994 NCOs and other ranks
Wounded: 947 officers, 33,257 NCOs and other ranks

Calendar of battles and engagements

14.08 – 19.08.1914	Battles in the Vosges
14.08 – 19.08.1914	In the Vallée de la Bruche
20.08 – 22.08.1914	Battle in the mid-Vosges region
22.08 – 14.09.1914	Battle for Nancy – Épinal
26.09 – 06.10.1914	Battle of the Somme
07.10 – 10.10.1914	Trench warfare west of Saint-Quentin
10.10.1914 – 23.06.1916	Trench warfare in the Artois west of Bapaume
17.12 – 18.12.1914	Battle of Ovillers – La Boisselle
07.06 – 13.06.1915	Battle of Serre
24.06 – 26.11.1916	Battle of the Somme
27.11.1916 – 15.03.1917	Trench warfare on the Somme
16.03 – 11.05.1917	Fighting on the Siegfried front
12.04 – 28.04.1917	Battle of Arras
18.05 – 11.08.1917	Positional battles in Flanders and Artois
11.08 – 18.09.1917	Battle in Flanders
19.09 – 11.10.1917	Training
13.10 – 03.12.1917	Battle in Flanders
04.12.1917 – 15.02.1918	Trench warfare in Flanders during the winter of 1917-18
15.02 – 11.03.1918	Border guards on the Belgian-Dutch border (GHQ reserve)
12.03 – 20.03.1918	Training
21.03 – 06.04.1918	March Offensive
21.03 – 23.03.1918	Breakthrough Battle Monchy – Cambrai
21.03 – 23.03.1918	Battle for the Mühlenberg

28.03.1918	Attack on the Scarpe
07.04 – 25.07.1918	Fighting between Arras and Albert
15.07 – 25.07.1918	Battle of Hébuterne
24.08 – 02.09.1918	Battle of Monchy – Bapaume
21.09 – 08.10.1918	Defensive battle between Cambrai and Saint-Quentin
09.10 – 04.11.1918	Fighting in front of and in the Hermann position
24.10 – 04.11.1918	Battle of Valenciennes
05.11 – 11.11.1918	Fighting retreat to the Antwerp – Meuse position
12.11 – 08.12.1918	Evacuation of the occupied territory and the march home

Bibliography

http://www.militaerpass.net. Orders of battle and pre-1918
German units overview.
US Government. *Histories of Two Hundred and Fifty-One Divisions which
participated in the war (1914-1918)*. Washington. 1920.

Index of places

Index of People, Equipment and Units